Lives and Times

J.L. Kraft

The Founder of Kraft Foods

Rebecca Vickers

Heinemann Library
Chicago, Illinois

Customer Service 888-454-2279
Visit our website at www.heinemannlibrary.com

Designed by Richard Parker and Maverick Design
Photo research by Julie Laffin
Printed and bound in China by South China Printing Company Limited

09 08 07 06 05
10 9 8 7 6 5 4 3 2 1

Library of Congress Cataloging-in-Publication Data
Vickers, Rebecca.
    J.L. Kraft / Rebecca Vickers.
        p. cm. -- (Lives and times)
    Includes bibliographical references and index.
    ISBN 1-4034-6344-1 (lib. bdg.) -- ISBN 1-4034-6358-1 (pbk.)
1. Kraft, James Lewis, 1874-1953--Juvenile literature. 2. Kraft Foods Company--Biography--Juvenile literature. 3. Cheese industry--United States--Biography--Juvenile literature. 4. Industrialists--United States--Biography--Juvenile literature. I. Title. II. Series: Lives and times (Des Plaines, Ill.)
    HD9280.U62K738 2005
    338.7'6373'092--dc22

                            2004021937

Acknowledgments
The author and publishers are grateful to the following for permission to reproduce copyright material:
p. 4 Image Bank Film/Getty Images; pp. 5, 7, 13, 14, 18, 19, 20, 21, 22, 23, 25, 26 Kraft Foods Inc.; p. 6, 17 The Granger Collection; pp. 8, 9, 10, 11, 12, 16 Corbis; p. 8 North Wind Picture Archives; p. 15 W.K. Kellogg Foundation; p. 24 Andrew E. Cook; p. 27 David McNew/Getty Images

Cover photographs by Kraft Foods Inc.

Cover and interior icons Janet Lankford Moran/Heinemann Library

Every effort has been made to contact copyright holders of any material reproduced in this book. Any omissions will be rectified in subsequent printings if notice is given to the publishers.

Some words are shown in bold, **like this**. You can find out what they mean by looking in the glossary.

Contents

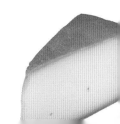

From Fresh to Processed

Fresh food is good for you. **Refrigeration** keeps some foods fresh, but over time **bacteria** grows. This can make food go bad.

Fresh cheese is very tasty, but it can easily go bad.

James Lewis Kraft was a cheese seller. He wanted to find a way to make food last longer. He built up a big **business**, **processing** cheese and other foods.

J.L. Kraft and his **company invented** many **convenience foods**.

The Early Years

James Lewis Kraft (called J.L.) was born November 11, 1874, near Lake Erie in Ontario, Canada. His parents were George and Minerva Kraft.

These are early photographs of J.L.'s parents.

The home where J.L. grew up would have looked like this one.

J.L. was the second of eleven children.
His father was a farmer.

Working Hard

J.L.'s family was very religious. They believed in the Bible and lived very simple lives.

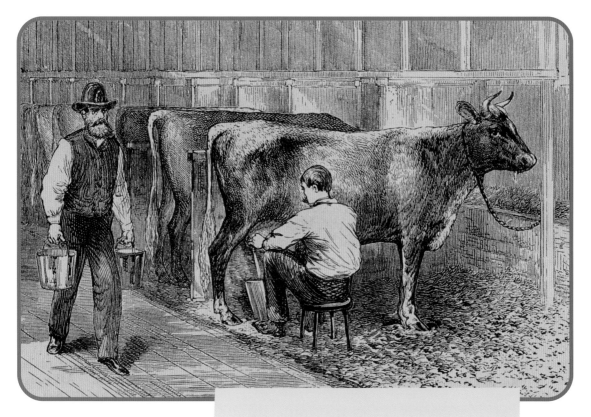

J.L. and his family lived and worked on a dairy farm like this one.

In most small towns, the general store was the only place to buy things.

J.L. went to the local high school and worked hard to help his father. His first job was as a clerk at Ferguson's **General Store** in Fort Erie.

Crossing the Border

J.L. worked at Ferguson's for about ten years. In 1902 he moved across the border to the United States. He became a **partner** in a cheese **company** in Buffalo, New York.

Buffalo was much bigger than the small town in Canada where J.L. had been living.

J.L. left Buffalo to work for the company in Chicago, Illinois. Sadly for J.L., his partners turned against him. He ended up in Chicago with no job and only $65!

In the early 1900s, Chicago was the second largest city in the United States.

Trading in Cheese

In Chicago J.L. started to buy and sell cheese. He bought good cheese very early in the morning from the South Water Street **market.**

Grocery store owners liked buying from J.L. It meant they did not have to get up early to go to a market like this one.

J.L. first sold his cheese to grocery stores from a horse-drawn wagon.

By 1914 the **company** sold 30 kinds of cheese across the United States. Four of J.L.'s brothers came to work for him. He started the J.L. Kraft and Brothers Company in 1909.

A Wife and a Daughter

In 1910 J.L. married Pauline Elizabeth Platt. In 1916 J.L. and Pauline had a baby daughter, Edith.

This picture shows J.L. and Pauline with their daughter, Edith.

At the same time, W.K. Kellogg, the cereal maker (seen here), also tried to keep foods fresh.

Soon after his marriage, J.L. became a **citizen** of the United States. He was also working hard to find a way to keep cheese from going bad.

Cheese Goes to War

In 1914 **World War I** started in Europe. The United States joined the war in 1917. U.S. soldiers needed healthy food **rations**.

Americans going off to war meant more **business** for Kraft and Brothers.

The U.S. **government** bought six million pounds of Kraft's canned cheese during World War I.

J.L. had worked out a way to **process** cheese to keep it fresh. The army thought Kraft's canned processed cheese would be perfect for the soldiers to eat.

Processing and Patents

J.L.'s **company** made special **pasteurized** cheese that lasted a long time. Over the years, Kraft and Brothers took out many **patents** so that no one could steal their ideas.

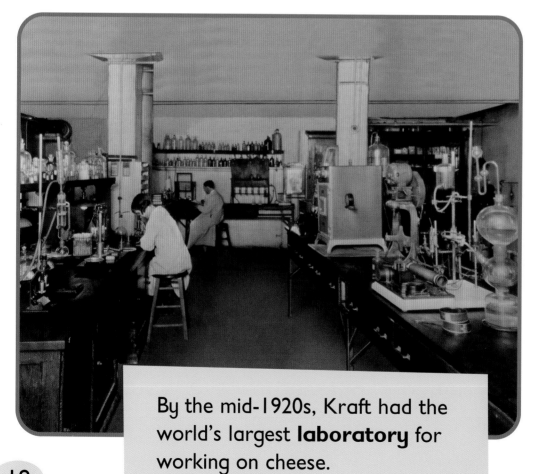

By the mid-1920s, Kraft had the world's largest **laboratory** for working on cheese.

Another company, Phenix Cheese, also made **processed** cheese. The two companies joined in 1928 to form the Kraft-Phenix Cheese Corporation.

The Phenix Cheese Company was famous for its *Philadelphia Cream Cheese.*

Advertising and Entertainment

J.L. Kraft believed in **advertising**. At the beginning, he used local newspapers. When the **company** got bigger, it advertised in national magazines.

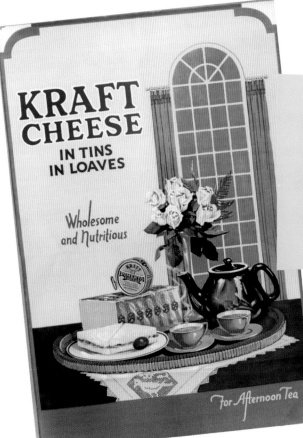

Kraft products were advertised to show how they could be used.

"Kraft Television Theater" was shown on television from 1947 to 1958.

In the 1930s, Kraft **sponsored** a radio program called "Kraft Music Hall." Later, the company sponsored the first big television drama program, "Kraft Television Theatre."

Kraft Foods

The Kraft-Phenix Cheese Corporation grew quickly. By the early 1930s, it had 10,000 workers in 30 states and 4 other countries.

By the 1940s, Kraft made much more than cheese. It changed its name to Kraft Foods.

One of the most famous Kraft products, *Velveeta*, was **invented** in 1928. *Miracle Whip* and *Kraft Macaroni and Cheese Dinner* went on sale in the 1930s.

Kraft Macaroni and Cheese Dinner is still one of Kraft's most popular products.

After the War

By 1945 J.L. Kraft was a very successful man. He still made time for his hobby, collecting a green stone called **jade**. He collected jade from all over the world.

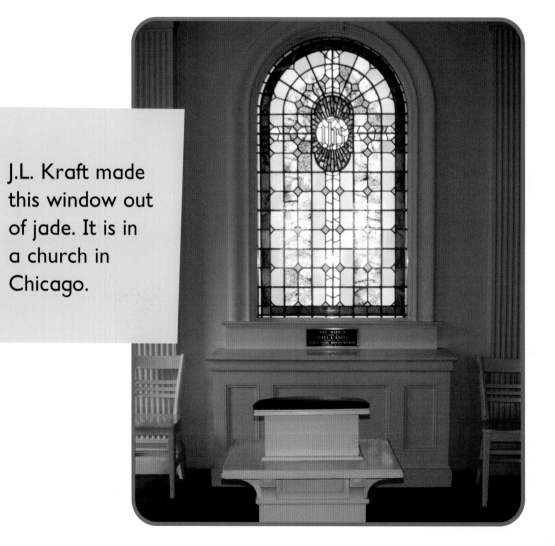

J.L. Kraft made this window out of jade. It is in a church in Chicago.

J.L. stopped working for Kraft Foods in 1951. He died in Chicago on February 16, 1953, when he was 78 years old.

This is a photograph of J.L. in his later years.

More About J.L.

J.L. Kraft was more than just successful at **inventing** and **business**. He was good to his workers, and he gave away a lot of his money.

J.L. and Pauline worked together to make life better for other people.

Today Kraft Foods products are made and sold all around the world. There are Kraft Food businesses in more than 150 countries.

Starting with only cheese, Kraft Foods now sells coffee, chocolate, cereal, cookies, and many other foods.

Fact File

- J.L.'s parents spelled their name "Krafft." J.L. changed it so that it was spelled with just one "f."

- The U.S. **government** bought Kraft **processed** cheese to use in **rations** for soldiers.

- J.L. was an expert on the valuable stone, **jade**. His book on jade was published in 1947.

- One of the most popular foods in Australia, the spread *Vegemite*, is a Kraft product.

- Kraft Foods still sells more cheese than any other **company** in the world.

Timeline

1874	James L. Kraft is born on November 11
1902	J.L. leaves Canada for Buffalo, New York
1903	J.L. moves to Chicago, Illinois
1909	J.L. Kraft and Brothers Company is set up
1910	J.L. marries Pauline Elizabeth Platt
1911	J.L. becomes a U.S. **citizen**
1916	J.L. Kraft and Brothers takes out first **patents** on cheese processing
1919	The first color **advertising** of Kraft products in national magazines
1928	Kraft Cheese Company and Phenix Cheese Company become the Kraft-Phenix Cheese Corporation
1945	Company name becomes Kraft Foods Company
1951	J.L. hands over job as head of Kraft Foods to his younger brother, John
1953	James L. Kraft dies on February 16

Glossary

advertising telling people about something

bacteria very small living things

business activity that earns money

citizen official member of a country

company group of people who make money by selling things

convenience food food that is easy to use

general store store that sells everything

government group that leads the country and makes laws

invent make something that has never been made before

jade hard green stone

laboratory where scientific work is carried out

market where people buy or sell things

partners owners of a company

pasteurized heated to kill bad bacteria

patent ownership of an idea or invention to so no one can copy it

processing method used to change something

rations packages of food for soldiers

refrigeration using cold to keep things fresh

sponsored paid to advertise

World War I war fought in Europe from 1914 to 1918

More Books to Read

Leeper, Angela. *Dairy Plant.* Chicago, IL: Heinemann Library, 2004.

Zemlicka, Shannon. *From Milk to Cheese.* Minneapolis, MN: Learner Publishing Group, 2003.

Index